THE WORLD OF
CASTLES AND FORTS

MALCOLM DAY

PETER BEDRICK BOOKS

NEW YORK

Published in the United States in 1999
by Peter Bedrick Books
A division of NTC/Contemporary
Publishing Group, Inc.
4255 West Touhy Avenue,
Lincolnwood (Chicago), Illinois
60646-1975 U.S.A.

Copyright © Macdonald Young
Books Ltd 1995

Library of Congress Cataloging-in-
   Publication Data
Day, Malcolm.
    [Keep out]
    The world of castles and
    forts/Malcolm Day.
       p.   cm.
    Originally published: Keep out!
Hemel Hempstead, Herts
Macdonald Young Books Ltd., 1995.
    Includes index.
    Summary: An illustrated history of
castles and forts through the ages, from
Mycenaean citadels to bomb shelters.
    ISBN 0-87226-278-2
    1. Fortification—Juvenile literature.
2. Castles—Juvenile literature.   [1.
Castles.   2. Fortification.]   I. Title.
UG401.D28 1996
355.7'09—dc20   96-31619
                               CIP
                               AC

Printed and Bound in Portugal by
Edições ASA

International Standard Book
Number: 0-87226-278-2

99 00 01 02 03 15 14 13 12 11 10 9 8 7 6 5 4 3

CONTENTS

Words in **bold** are explained in
the glossary on page 44.

SAFE FROM ATTACK

From early times, people have built protection around them. Stone Age people lived in caves and made fences to keep out wild animals. The first cities, such as Jericho, which was built around 10,000 BC, had high stone walls to keep out invaders. Kings and nobles fortified their large homes to protect themselves even against their own people.

Castles became so strong by the Middle Ages that the only way to seize them was by trickery. Then came gunpowder and everything began to change. As the science of artillery developed, so the castle with its high vertical walls became out of date. Cleverer designs of fortification were made to withstand heavy bombardment. By the time of World War II, a fortress was even built underground.

Today, forts are no longer built because bombs are too powerful. In an age when nuclear bombs can destroy whole states, fortification is more a matter of computer control. Highly sophisticated radars, satellites and lasers interact to prevent rockets hitting their targets. Nations now hide their military installations from enemy view. So from the time when fortresses stood out proudly on high ground, such as the Crusader castle, Krak des Chevaliers, we have now progressed to the idea of 'invisible defense'.

CITADELS OF THE GIANTS

The cities of the ancient Mycenaeans seem unbelievable. In fact, the walls of these great **citadels** were so massive that later Greeks believed they were built by the legendary giants, called the Cyclops. Enormous blocks of stone were piled together to form walls several yards thick. These walls surrounded cities built on high ground. From here, powerful warrior kings ruled over the land and often went to war with neighboring states.

The Mycenaeans lived in Greece during the Bronze Age (c. 4000–2000 BC). Their capital city was Mycenae, which had a palace rich with treasures. Golden masks of dead heroes tell the tale of great battles. One such tale was that a Mycenaean king by the name of Agamemnon destroyed the great city of Troy in the Trojan War.

Mycenae was a city of great wealth and prestige. The palace stood proudly overlooking the tiny dwellings of peasants who made weapons for an elite band of warriors. The strongest warrior became king and when he died in battle a gold death mask was made in his likeness. The mask above was thought to be of Agamemnon, who led his people in the Trojan War.

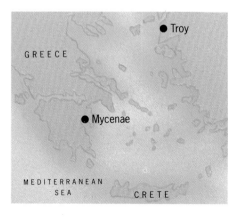

THE MIGHTY LION GATE

*Massive walls, as thick as 30 feet, protected the inhabitants of Mycenae. The only entrance was by the Lion Gate, so-called because two carved lions stood over the doorway. Guards in the **watchtower** warned of enemy approach and soldiers on the wall could throw spears and stones at attackers. To the right of the gate was the grave circle where dead rulers and heroes were buried.*

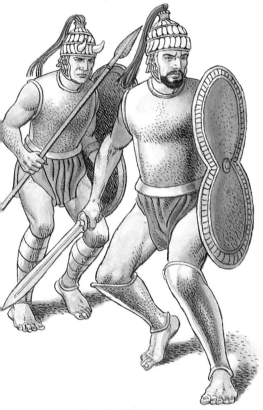

THE WOODEN HORSE OF TROY

A famous enemy of the ancient Greeks were the Trojans. Their city of Troy was so strong that after ten years of siege the Greeks could only capture it by trickery. Pretending to retreat, they left behind a wooden horse. The Trojans believed it to be a gift, and took it inside their walls. At nightfall, Greek soldiers, who had been hiding in the belly of the horse, climbed down and opened the gates for the waiting army.

Mycenaeans fought with daggers and spears made of bronze. Their shields were shaped in a figure of eight so that they could easily move them in combat. Some soldiers carried larger shields which could also serve as stretchers for the wounded.

THE GRAVE CIRCLE

Inside the Lion Gate, to the right, was the grave circle. Five graves have been found here, holding 15 skeletons of rulers and their families. They were buried with gold and personal belongings, including golden funerary masks.

THE SIEGE OF LACHISH

I n 701 BC, King Sennacherib of the Assyrians invaded Judah, a little kingdom to the east of the Mediterranean Sea. The Assyrians were a powerful and cruel people from the mountainous north. Surrounding kingdoms trembled at the thought of what they might do. With terrifying force, Sennacherib attacked 47 cities in Judah. The Bible described him as like a wolf coming down on a fold of sheep.

The people of Judah needed to defend themselves as best they could. The strongest fortified city was Lachish. Soldiers were stationed along its high walls and towers that looked over the countryside of vineyards and olive trees. Some 300 yards away, out of arrow range, the Assyrians set up camp. For many months, perhaps even more than a year, they besieged (continuously attacked) the city. After a long struggle the inhabitants of Lachish surrendered - exhausted, hungry and with no weapons left to use against the enemy.

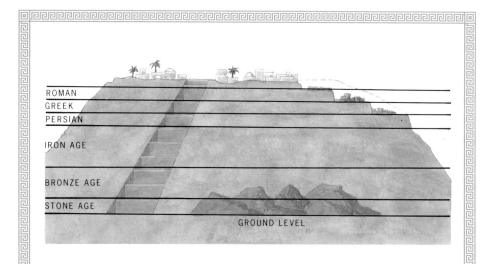

BELOW THE SURFACE

M any cities in Judah were built on a mound. When invading armies destroyed a city, a new one would be built on top. The diagram above shows how the mound has risen from one civilization to the next, from the Stone Age to the Romans. The city of Lachish belonged to the late Iron Age. If you could cut vertically through the mound, like a cake, you would see layers of earth (right) with buried pots and bones.

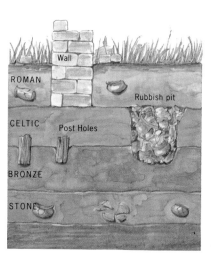

THE ASSYRIAN SIEGE MACHINE

The Assyrians had powerful siege engines to break down the walls of cities. The lower section contained a battering ram manned by attackers inside. Archers shot arrows from the top story to gain equal height with defenders on the wall. The machine was very heavy and was usually hauled into place by oxen.

Before attacking a city, the Assyrians would offer peace in return for surrender. If refused, they would build a ramp of wood and earth, and wheel up their battering rams to breach the wall. Bowmen and slingers shot at defenders on the walls. They retaliated by throwing down missiles and flaming torches which would set fire to the wooden battering rams.

IRON AGE FORTS

Between about 500 BC and the time of the Romans, the people of northern Europe built forts on hills. This was the Iron Age. Tools, weapons and chariot wheels could now be made of iron. Villages or large farming camps were set up on high ground to avoid floods and to defend them easily. They dug the earth up and made **ramparts** to circle the village. A wooden fence enclosed thatched huts and kept in farm animals.

At this time there were no long-range weapons. Men threw spears and stones, and later the sling was invented. But most fighting was hand to hand. Julius Caesar described an attack on a hill fort in north France: 'The attackers surround the whole circuit of the wall with a large number of men, and shower stones at it from all sides. When they have cleared it of defenders, they lock their shields over their heads, advance close up, and undermine it [dig under and cause the wall to collapse].'

An aerial view of the ancient site of Maiden Castle in England shows the remains of the earth ramparts that surrounded the fort. This was one of the largest of the Iron Age forts in Europe, and was destroyed by the Romans in AD 44 after a battle at the eastern gate.

Maiden Castle is besieged at the eastern gate. It is protected by a maze of ramparts and ditches. Defenders on top of the ramparts hurl stones and javelins at the bewildered attackers, who are trying to find the entrance to the fort.

Life in the hill fort was usually quiet. Thatched huts, the size of an average two-bedroomed bungalow, housed farmers, tool-makers and wood-cutters. Some huts were granaries for storing wheat, others were stables for horses used in chariot racing and hunting. Near the center of the compound was the chieftain's hut with a large courtyard where the whole community could be assembled at times of emergency, such as the threat of an enemy attack.

THE SLINGSHOT THEORY

By about the third century BC, the sling appeared in Britain. It could hurl a pebble accurately over 150 yards. The archaeologist Sir Mortimer Wheeler had a theory that defenders built ramparts to keep the enemy 00 yards away. At this distance, defenders standing on e high ground could hit the enemy, but their stones could t reach the defenders. Maiden Castle exactly meets these quirements. An ammunition store of 20,000 beach bbles was found at the site.

RAMPARTS FOR DEFENSE

A rampart was made of earth dug out of a **ditch** in front of it. Charging attackers would be slowed down by having to go into the ditch and then climb the sloping bank or **glacis** of the rampart. Defenders lay waiting behind a wooden **palisade** (fence) at the top. More advanced defenses (center and right below) had a raised earth platform behind a high palisade to give defenders an even greater height advantage over the enemy.

Glacis type with palisade

Revetted earth rampart piled behind palisade

Timber laced rampart

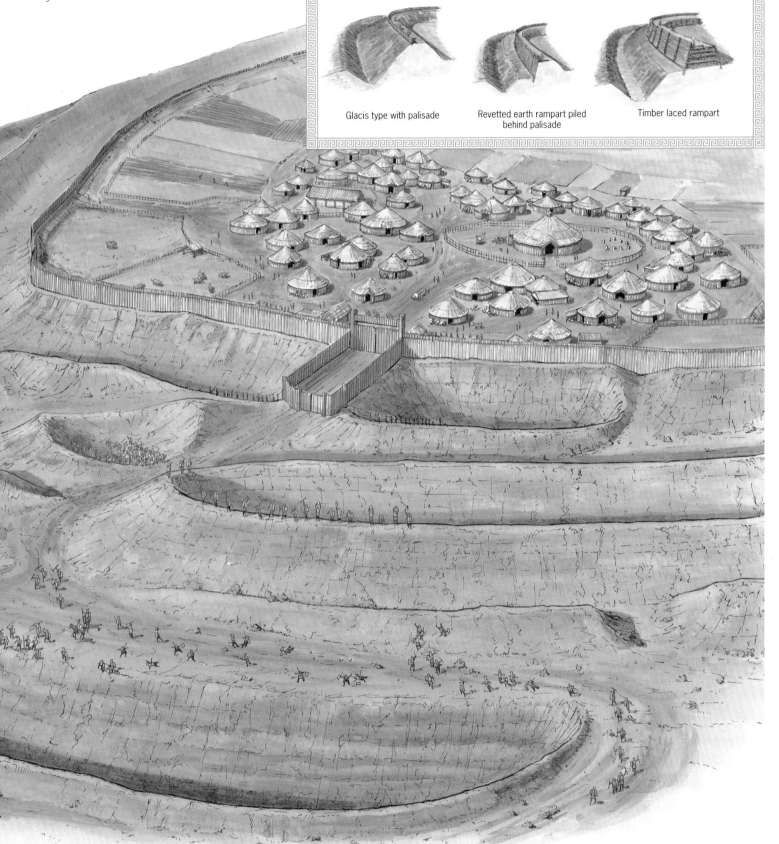

THE GREAT WALL

From the coast of China, east of Beijing (Peking), right into the distant deserts of Asia, runs the Great Wall of China. It snakes over mountains and through valleys like a monster dragon. A guard on watch in the eighth century AD described roads disappearing into the sky, and 1,000 miles (1,600 km) of moonlight on the wall. But all the time danger lurked in the surrounding sands.

The Wall was not always one continuous line. In earliest times, small kingdoms in China built walls to keep out hostile nomads from the north. When China became a united empire under the Ch'in rulers (221-206 BC), separate walls were joined together to form one continuous wall along the northern border of China. The Han emperors (206 BC-AD 220) added watchtowers and beacons to send fire and smoke signals to warn the emperor of invasion.

The Ming rulers (1368-1644) built most of the Wall which stands today. This was a much stronger construction made of stone. Slaves were forced to build it with their bare hands, and thousands died of hunger and exhaustion.

The map above shows the Great Wall during the period of the Ming emperors of China (1368-1644). Building the Wall was hard labor. Long, hot days were spent carrying stones, bricks and timber for construction. Two stone walls, 30 feet high, were filled with rubble and pounded earth. On this was laid a brick road for messengers to gallop along on horseback.

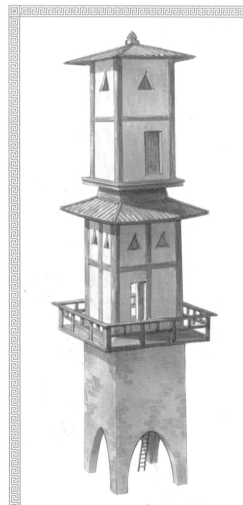

THE WATCHTOWERS

Defensive watchtowers, like this clay model, were common in China. They guarded against robbers on the estates of large houses and even in the burial grounds of emperors. The watchtowers of the Great Wall, however, were much larger, usually about 40 feet high. They could house troops and weapons, animal pens and brushwood for making fires, and food supplies for the long periods of watching over the landscape. On sight of an enemy, the duty guards raised the alarm by signaling to neighboring watchtowers, by smoke during the day and by fire at night. Soldiers stationed at other sections of the wall were summoned to the scene of attack. They could cover large distances of difficult terrain quickly by galloping along the flat top of the Wall.

Slaves could earn their freedom by working on the Wall and peasant farmers who had lost their land would also come here. A special community grew up. Some parts of the Wall were so far from civilization that food had to be grown as best it could in the poor soil. Other activities here included trading grain for salt with nomads.

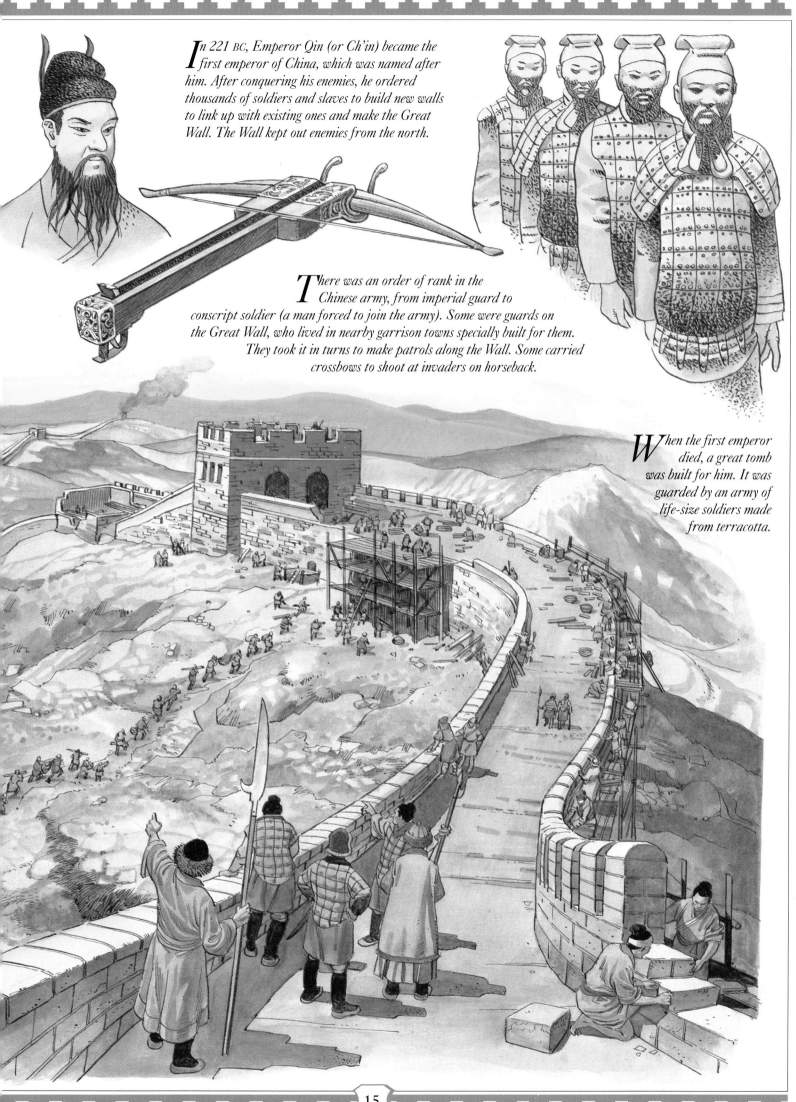

In 221 BC, Emperor Qin (or Ch'in) became the first emperor of China, which was named after him. After conquering his enemies, he ordered thousands of soldiers and slaves to build new walls to link up with existing ones and make the Great Wall. The Wall kept out enemies from the north.

There was an order of rank in the Chinese army, from imperial guard to conscript soldier (a man forced to join the army). Some were guards on the Great Wall, who lived in nearby garrison towns specially built for them. They took it in turns to make patrols along the Wall. Some carried crossbows to shoot at invaders on horseback.

When the first emperor died, a great tomb was built for him. It was guarded by an army of life-size soldiers made from terracotta.

THE FORTRESS OF MASADA

A huge rock in the Judean Desert, the area of 18 football fields, towers as high as the Empire State Building in New York. On one side lies the Dead Sea, on the other a vast desert that looks more like the moon than anywhere on earth. Upon this rock Herod the Great built one of the world's most spectacular fortresses. It became the last stronghold of the Jews in their resistance to the Romans during the Jewish War of AD 66-73.

In AD 66 Jewish Zealots, who wanted to overthrow Roman rule in Palestine, occupied Masada. After the fall of Jerusalem, the Romans hunted down all fleeing Jews until they arrived at Masada. The Romans set up camp and built a high fence circling the rock to prevent the Jews smuggling in food and water supplies. Because the fortress walls were so high, the Romans built a ramp made of earth.

Up the ramp the Romans hauled a siege tower from which they could set fire to the fortress wall. After two years of siege, they were ready for the final assault. With no hope left, the 960 defending Jews decided overnight to kill themselves rather than allow the Romans that pleasure. Only seven women and children survived to tell the tale.

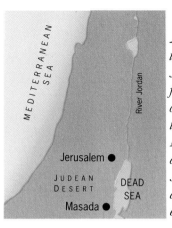

Herod the Great (king of Judea from 40 BC to 4 BC) was hated by the Jews because he was a friend of the Romans. In case of trouble, he decided to build a fortress at Masada. It had a strong defensive site, with the Judean Desert to the west and the Dead Sea to the east.

Herod the Great turned a rock in the wilderness into a walled fortress. At the north end, a palace-villa almost hung from the cliff, with a sheer drop of 1300 feet to the shore of the Dead Sea below. Built on three levels, the palace commanded magnificent views across the Dead Sea and up the Jordan Valley. Steps hollowed through the cliffs connected the luxurious columned pavilions, where Herod entertained in safety. His fortifications and the ingenious water sytem his architects designed enabled the Jews to hold out for two years during the Roman siege.

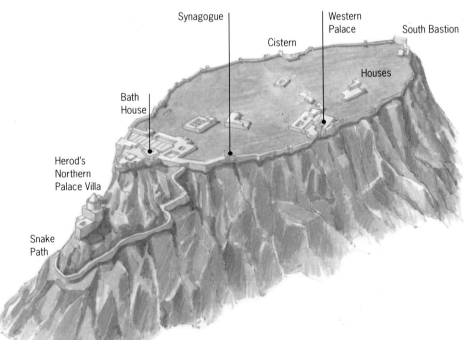

PLAN OF HEROD'S FORTRESS

The plan shows Masada from the west side. The Dead Sea was on the other side. The only access was by the snake path, seen in the foreground. At the top, a whole community could live: the royal family in palaces, priests in smaller houses, and soldiers in the **barracks**.

There were also chambers set within the double walls that surrounded the summit. A synagogue held religious ceremonies and store-rooms kept large supplies of food. Among the items found after the siege were leather sandals, baskets, bronze pans and jugs, and woolen prayer shawls.

ROMAN SOLDIER

The Roman army consisted of legionaries (foot soldiers) and their commanders, known as centurions. The centurion (pictured right) was always chosen from Romans who had proved themselves to be reliable and determined. He led 100 legionaries into battle. His uniform included a leather kilt and cuirass (an armored chest garment). Bronze greaves protected shins and knees, and a crested helmet protected the head. The centurion carried a dagger and two swords for fighting. He wore a smart robe as a mark of his rank.

ROMAN SIEGE TOWER

The Romans developed the siege tower from the cruder type used by the ancient Assyrians. Once wheeled into place, usually hauled by animals, the tower operated at several levels. It dropped a **drawbridge** on to the top of a citadel's walls for soldiers to cross when they had cleared away defenders. At the base, soldiers could pull back a battering ram, suspended like a pendulum, and swing it with great force into the enemy wall. When the wall collapsed, soldiers poured through the breach at whichever level. At Masada, the tower provided a platform from which to set fire to the defenses.

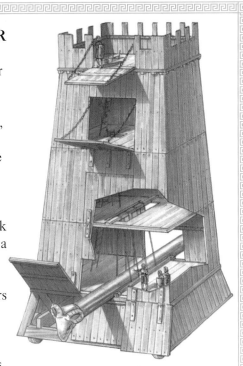

The Romans built a massive earth ramp, 200 yards long and 100 yards high, in order to besiege Masada. The Roman commander, Flavius Silva, conducted operations from below, on horseback. Legionaries marched up to fight, while catapults bombarded the walls.

FORTS OF THE EMPIRE

It took hundreds of years for the Romans to build their vast empire, which extended from Egypt to Britain. At times of unrest, they had to go long distances to defend their frontiers. They used to set up fortified marching camps at the end of each day's march. Up to 40,000 legionaries would follow a particular routine, each with his own task. They could build a complete fortified camp in a few hours, including tents, ditches and spiked fencing for protection.

The permanent forts which the Romans built along the frontiers of the empire were the same in layout. Wooden barracks replaced the tents and look-out towers were built at each corner. They were not designed to withstand attack, but were bases for garrisons of soldiers to go out and fight in open combat. There was a gate positioned on each side so that the soldiers could make quick exits.

The Roman Empire reached its maximum size in abou AD 117, under Emperor Trajan. The Romans built cavalry forts, like the one shown, to defend the frontiers of the empire. The headquarters surrounded a central courtyard. Barracks housed the legionaries. Other buildings were stables for the cavalry horses, a hospital, granary, storehouse, work shops and lavatories. Outside the compound was a bath-house, used regularly by the Romans.

The Romans used sophisticated weapons in battle. One of the deadliest in both defense and attack was the ballista (a kind of catapult), shown above. It could accurately shoot long arrows or stones weighing up to 50 lb. The operator could position the ballista at different angles by adjusting the rachet below. He turned the windlass and the two front arms were turned backwards by a twisting rope. A trigger then released the mechanism and shot the missile a distance of up to 1300 feet (¹⁄₄ mile).

A Roman Gatehouse

Roman forts and fortified towns throughout the empire had **gatehouses**, made of stone or brick. Later builders of castles in the Dark Ages of Europe copied the Roman structure of an arched gateway between two towers. A gatehouse provided living quarters for the guard who operated the gates. Iron plating and raw hides sometimes covered the wooden gates to protect them from fire. Inner staircases led up to the second level where soldiers could man the **parapets** that topped the fort wall.

Under the supervision of a prefect, it was the legionary troops who built the forts. The legion (6,000 foot soldiers) had a wide range of skilled men, including architects, carpenters, stone-cutters, glaziers, roof-tile makers, plumbers and ditch-diggers. They looked after their own tools, some shown with the legionary below.

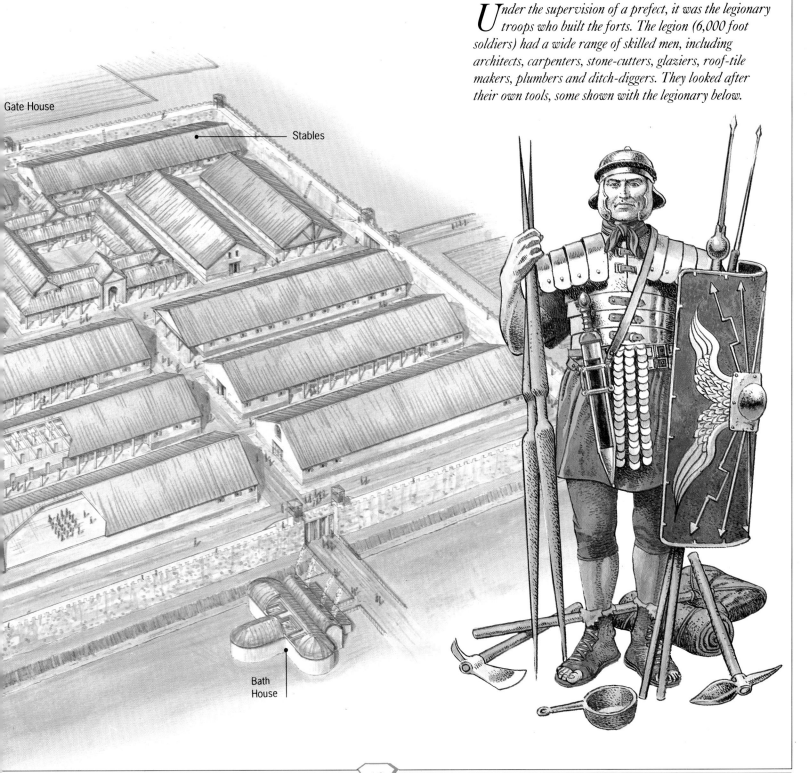

Gate House

Stables

Bath House

THE NORMAN CONQUEST

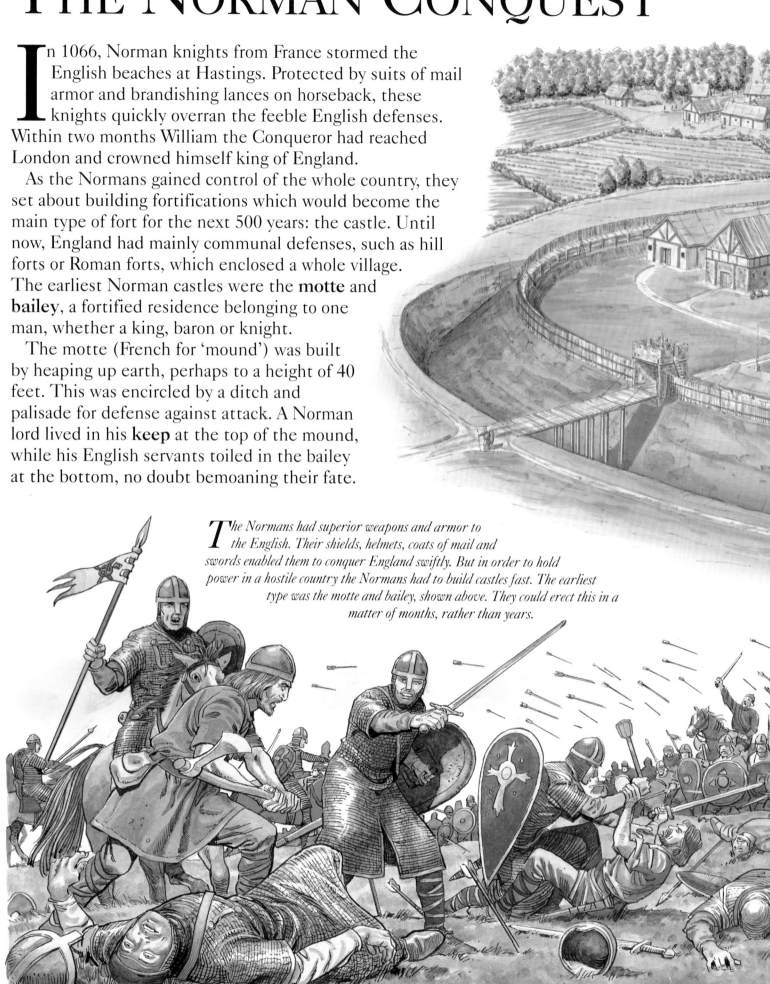

In 1066, Norman knights from France stormed the English beaches at Hastings. Protected by suits of mail armor and brandishing lances on horseback, these knights quickly overran the feeble English defenses. Within two months William the Conqueror had reached London and crowned himself king of England.

As the Normans gained control of the whole country, they set about building fortifications which would become the main type of fort for the next 500 years: the castle. Until now, England had mainly communal defenses, such as hill forts or Roman forts, which enclosed a whole village. The earliest Norman castles were the **motte** and **bailey**, a fortified residence belonging to one man, whether a king, baron or knight.

The motte (French for 'mound') was built by heaping up earth, perhaps to a height of 40 feet. This was encircled by a ditch and palisade for defense against attack. A Norman lord lived in his **keep** at the top of the mound, while his English servants toiled in the bailey at the bottom, no doubt bemoaning their fate.

The Normans had superior weapons and armor to the English. Their shields, helmets, coats of mail and swords enabled them to conquer England swiftly. But in order to hold power in a hostile country the Normans had to build castles fast. The earliest type was the motte and bailey, shown above. They could erect this in a matter of months, rather than years.

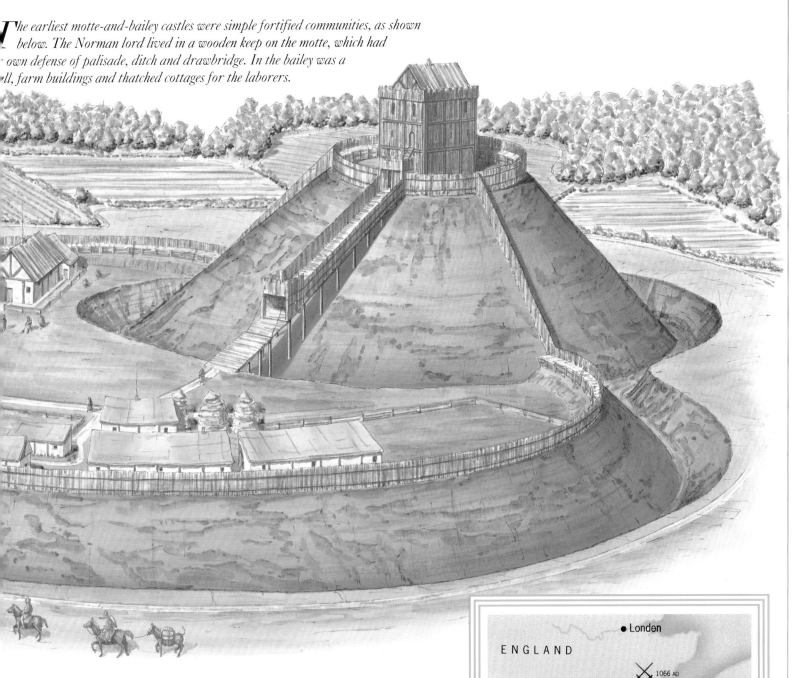

The earliest motte-and-bailey castles were simple fortified communities, as shown below. The Norman lord lived in a wooden keep on the motte, which had [its] own defense of palisade, ditch and drawbridge. In the bailey was a [hall], farm buildings and thatched cottages for the laborers.

THE ART OF THE WOOD-CUTTER

In the bailey lived craftsmen and women, such as tool-makers, [tan]ners and weavers. One [of] the most needed was the [wo]od-cutter, because most [str]uctures in the eleventh [ce]ntury were wooden. He [no]t felled trees to make [pa]lisade fences, towers, the [dr]awbridge, roof timbers, [do]ors, floors and furniture. [He] also made wooden [sc]affolding for roof [re]pairs, perhaps needed [aft]er a battle.

BATTLE OF HASTINGS, 1066

William of Normandy (north France) invaded England with an army of just 7,000 men (tiny compared with the Romans' 40,000). But in four years they had conquered the country. Then they filled the land with castles to defend it from invaders, such as the Danes.

Norman Keeps

By 1100 (34 years after the Conquest), the Normans had built perhaps 500 castles in England. This great number was partly to prevent an English uprising, and partly to defend against possible invasions from the heirs of King Canute of Denmark.

The wooden, motte-and-bailey fort was quick and easy to put up, so it suited the Normans when they were conquering England. But these constructions were extremely vulnerable to attack by fire. Many were burned down. The Normans decided to build stronger and longer-lasting castles, this time in stone. A stone castle took several seasons, or even years, to build, depending on its size. Wealthy lords could afford to pay a guild of stone masons to build a huge, turreted castle, such as the Tower of London, completed in the 1090s.

The Stone Mason

Stone castles replaced the wooden ones that burned down during battles. The stone mason was the craftsman who cut the stone to the right shape. If it was soft enough, like limestone, he could use a saw; for harder stone he used a chisel and hammer, like the man above in the background. Laborers brought boulders of stone from a nearby quarry for masons to cut.

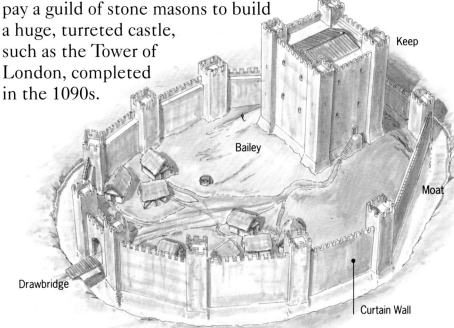

Keep

Bailey

Moat

Drawbridge

Curtain Wall

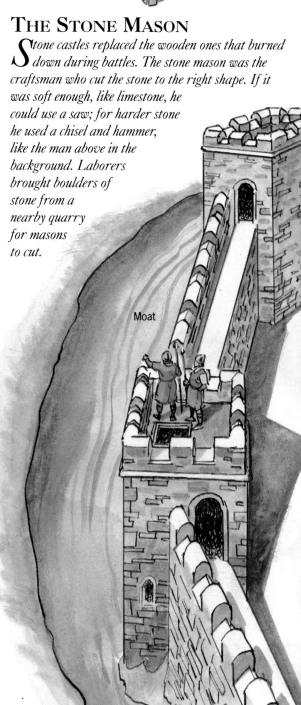

Moat

The Drawbridge

A drawbridge was a moveable bridge crossing the **moat** to the castle gate. Men in the gatehouse hauled up the drawbridge by chains, denying access to the enemy. Upstairs, men lowered an iron **portcullis**, which served as a second gate.

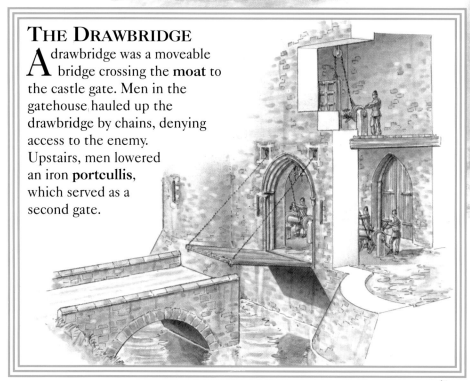

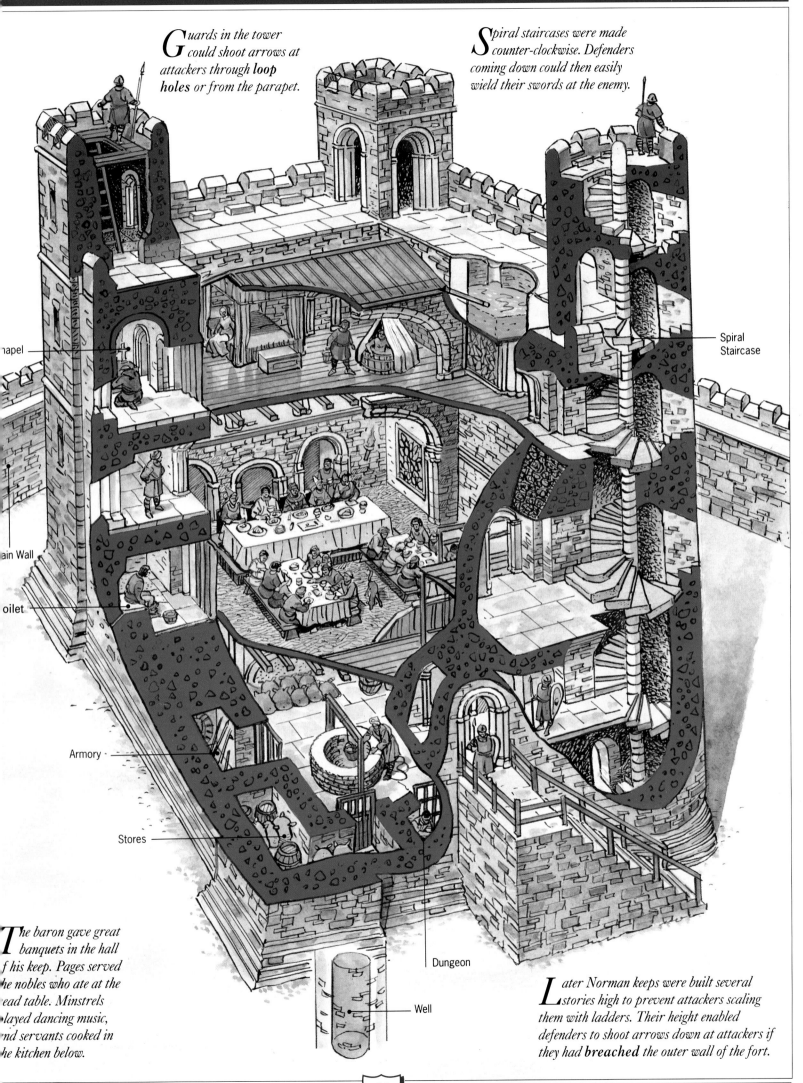

*G*uards in the tower could shoot arrows at attackers through **loop holes** or from the parapet.

*S*piral staircases were made counter-clockwise. Defenders coming down could then easily wield their swords at the enemy.

Spiral Staircase

Chapel

Main Wall

Toilet

Armory

Stores

Dungeon

Well

*T*he baron gave great banquets in the hall of his keep. Pages served the nobles who ate at the head table. Minstrels played dancing music, and servants cooked in the kitchen below.

*L*ater Norman keeps were built several stories high to prevent attackers scaling them with ladders. Their height enabled defenders to shoot arrows down at attackers if they had **breached** the outer wall of the fort.

KRAK DES CHEVALIERS

During the Middle Ages, the Christian powers of
Europe launched a series of attacks, or Crusades,
on Palestine - the Holy Land. Their aim was to free
Jerusalem and other holy places from the Arabs,
who practiced the religion of Islam. After initial success, the
Christians built castles to strengthen their grip on the lands
they had conquered. Their greatest fortress was Krak des
Chevaliers, stronghold of the Knights of St John. Built on
a hill above a fertile plain in Syria, the castle dominated the
surrounding countryside. After an earthquake in 1202, Krak
was redesigned, with two sets of massive walls punctuated
with towers. Finally, Krak fell in 1271, but only as a result of
trickery. The knights received a letter supposedly from their
commanders ordering them to surrender. But the
letter had been forged by the Arabs, who
took by cunning what
they could
not take
by force.

*The inner gate was defended by a portcullis
and a **machicolation** - a structure
projecting from the wall from which rocks or
boiling liquids could be dropped on to the
attackers below.*

Magazine
(below surface)

Great Hall
and Cloister

Chapel

Fosse
(Reservoir)

Machicolations

Sloped Walls
to prevent Mining

Lower
Main Gate

*Krak was similar
in style to the castles
of Europe which were being
built at the time. Two rings of
walls, towers and steep slopes
protected an inner courtyard where the
Grand Master, head of the knights of St John,
lived. The inner wall sloped outwards at its base to
prevent the enemy mining under it, making Krak one of
the most difficult fortresses in the world to capture.*

*The main outer gate, set in the eastern wall, could only be
approached up a sheer slope by a zigzag path, giving defenders
plenty of opportunity to hurl missiles at the advancing enemy.*

DEFENDERS OF THE FAITH

The Order of the Knights of St John was originally founded to provide inns and hospitals to Christian pilgrims traveling to the Holy Land. Hence their other name: the Knights Hospitallers. In time they developed into a military force ready to defend the faith anywhere in Christendom. They wore long tunics of black with a white cross on their chests which is still used today by the St John's Ambulance Association.

THE HOLY CRUSADES

The Crusades were holy wars started by Christians to recover the Holy Land, which was held by Muslims (followers of the religion of Islam). They began in 1095 at the suggestion of Pope Urban II, and lasted 200 years. In 1099, the Christians captured Jerusalem and established kingdoms east of the Mediterranean Sea. Krak des Chevaliers was one of the strongest castles built to defend their land.

The Crusaders fought many open battles against the Muslims, or Saracens, as they were known. However, they were at a disadvantage in fighting. The Saracens had smaller, quicker horses, and they carried light-weight curved swords called scimitars. These could be easily slashed at the Crusaders whose own swords were much heavier. As a result, the Crusaders lost more battles than they won. One of the most famous duels was fought between Richard the Lionheart and Saladin, leader of the Saracens.

THE PLANTAGENETS

The Plantagenets were English kings who succeeded the Normans. One of the most successful was Edward I (1272-1307). He was a soldier-king who fought a Crusade in the Holy Land. On his return to England, he set about building some gigantic castles in Wales.

The greatest of these castles was Harlech. Like Krak des Chevaliers, the site Edward chose was a high rocky crag. Two sides dropped over 200 feet sheer into the sea. The only possible side to attack it from was at the front. Here, a massive gatehouse (a fortress in itself) formed the heart of the defense, and was also the living quarters.

Plantagenet fortresses were a significant development from Norman times. Double wall belts, huge corner towers and turrets in the walls made them almost impossible to conquer. For 350 years Harlech remained intact, one of the strongest castles in Europe.

MINING A CASTLE

Before the age of gunpowder, one of the few ways attackers could capture a castle was by mining under the walls. Men dug a tunnel and supported its roof by wooden beams. When completed, they set fire to the wood, causing the tunnel and wall above it to collapse.

THE AGE OF CHIVALRY

Jousting at medieval tournaments was a mock battle performed during peacetime. Fighting became a noble art for knights who were ready to die for their lords and ladies.

Most castles had a garrison of knights who guarded against attack and also escorted their masters on journeys to protect them from robbers in the woods.

CONCENTRIC CASTLES

The Plantagenets who returned from the Crusades copied a new style of castle design, built mostly by the French. This was the concentric castle. It had several **lines of defense**, combining two or more **curtain walls** with any number of **bastions** and towers. This gave the keep more protection, and meant that attackers could only capture the fortress step by step. Notice the towers are now round, not square like Norman ones.

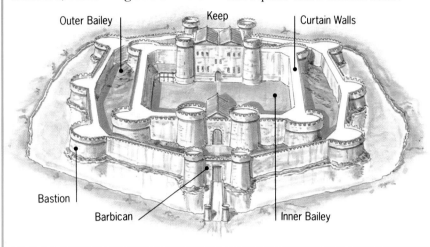

Outer Bailey · Keep · Curtain Walls · Bastion · Barbican · Inner Bailey

One of the most successful weapons of the Middle Ages was the trebuchet, shown above. Soldiers winched down a long arm with a sling at one end. On release, the sling could hurl a 300 lb. boulder to smash into walls as far away as 300 yards.

Harlech Castle was one of the strongest castles in medieval Europe. With sea on two sides, the only approach was from the front. The gatehouse, usually the weakest point of a castle, was here the strongest part, with huge round towers overlooking the moat and drawbridge. Not surprisingly, a large work force was used in building the castle: 115 stone quarriers, 227 stone masons, 30 metal-smiths, 22 carpenters and 546 laborers.

THE AGE OF ARTILLERY

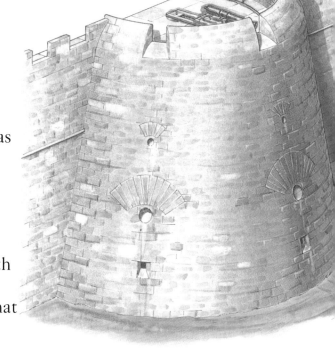

By the end of the 1300s gunpowder was widely in use. The medieval castle, with its high vertical walls, was no longer the invincible fortification it had been. Powerful iron cannons could now blast through its stone walls.

At first, existing castles were modified. Walls were thickened and sometimes covered with timber or earth to withstand the shock of cannon balls. But increasingly it was necessary to redesign and rebuild. The time of the Renaissance in Italy and France brought forward new thinkers, such as Leonardo da Vinci and Michelangelo, whose artistic inventions revolutionized the design of fortifications.

Circular or rectangular towers were replaced by ones with slanting sides to deflect shot. Walls were made lower and more sturdy. They were also built sloping backwards, so that striking cannon balls would fly over the top.

*T*he first ever design of a tank was drawn by Leonardo da Vinci. His circular armored vehicle, however, was never built.

*D*ürer (a German) designed the roundel (above). It was the shape of an upturned bucket which deflected attackers' cannon shot. Small **embrasures** in the walls were openings for gun barrels. At the top, a cannon moved on a carriage, enabling it to fire in different directions.

Ravelin

LEONARDO DA VINCI

*L*eonardo da Vinci was the outstanding engineer of the Renaissance. He developed the art of making cannons, improving their power and accuracy. He also made hundreds of designs of new styles of fortress, such as the one on the right. The walls are low and slope backwards to avoid receiving the full impact of a cannon ball, which is deflected up into the air.

INTRODUCING THE CANNON

The coming of gunpowder in the early 1300s marked the beginning of the end of the traditional medieval castle. In time, the iron cannon could be used by attackers to breach the vertical walls of castles. However, the earliest cannons were not very effective. They were heavy and only a few shots of rough stone balls could be fired, but without any great power. The force of the explosion, though, sometimes broke the cannon and killed the gunner!

Sarzanello in Italy marked a turning point in fortress design. Built in the fourteenth century, it was one of the first designed to withstand artillery fire. The thick splayed base (**talus**) deflected cannon balls and made undermining difficult. The left-hand end was an important new design feature, a **ravelin**, which made an attack on that side almost impossible.

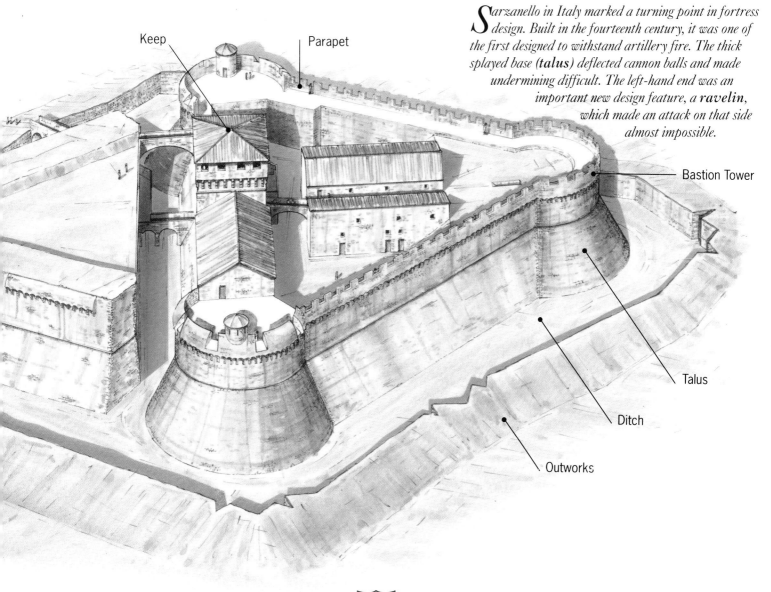

Keep

Parapet

Bastion Tower

Talus

Ditch

Outworks

HENRY VIII'S FORTS

Henry VIII (1509-1547) was not a popular man abroad. He had made enemies of France and Spain, and feared an invasion at any time. To defend his realm, he built 20 artillery forts along the coast from Kent to Cornwall during the 1530s.

Henry's masons used the roundel design of the German artist Albrecht Dürer, and developed what is known as the 'petalled' castle, because it looks like the petals of a flower. The largest of these forts was at Deal. Cannons on wheeled carriages could be speedily maneuvered inside, and on top of, low round bastions. As attacking ships sailed by, so cannons could follow them round.

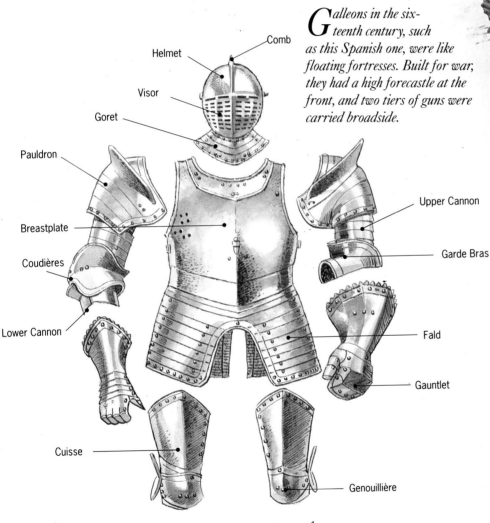

Helmet
Comb
Visor
Goret
Pauldron
Breastplate
Coudières
Lower Cannon
Upper Cannon
Garde Bras
Fald
Gauntlet
Cuisse
Genouillière

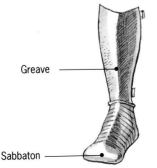

Greave
Sabbaton

Galleons in the sixteenth century, such as this Spanish one, were like floating fortresses. Built for war, they had a high forecastle at the front, and two tiers of guns were carried broadside.

Henry VIII's suit of armor was much heavier and gave more protection than the earlier armor of medieval knights. It consisted of many parts so that the wearer could move easily in combat. The metal armor was highly decorated and bore the knight's family heraldry.

Deal was the grandest of Henry's coastal forts. Semi-circular bastions surrounded a central keep. Long-range cannons on carriages fired from the roofs, and handguns were used at low levels - a total of 145 gunports all round

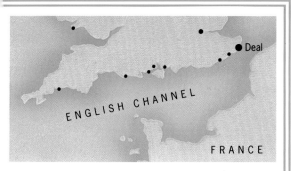

TUDOR COASTAL DEFENSES

From Kent to Cornwall, Tudor monarchs built artillery forts to defend Britain's coastline from invasion. This was the first organized national defense. However, soon more powerful cannons could breach the walls, and new designs were needed.

MARTELLO TOWERS

Martello towers were built to defend England's coast from invasion by Napoleon of France. The design was based on Dürer's roundel. The cut-away drawing shows the main gun on a rotating platform. The solid roof was bomb-proof. Below were living quarters and store-rooms. The only way to enter was by climbing a ladder to a door at the middle level, on the right.

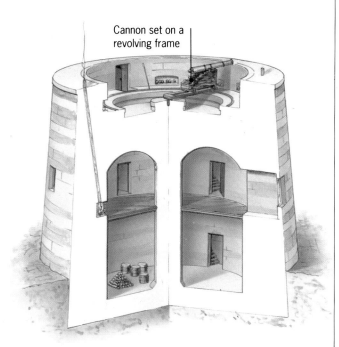

Cannon set on a revolving frame

HIMEJI CASTLE

The use of artillery in siege warfare was not confined to Europe. The Japanese discovered firearms when they boarded a Portuguese galleon that had washed up on their shores in 1542. By 1600 the Dutch and English were selling arms and ammunition to the Japanese shogun (military governor). As a result, castles in Japan, which until then were little more than shelters of wood and thatch, had to be rebuilt to withstand firepower.

One of these new castles was the White Heron Castle at Himeji (built in 1609). It was a hill-top fortress, enclosing a palace for the warlord (daimyo) and barracks for his Samurai warriors. The high, multi-story palace was designed to keep the lord as distant as possible from any disturbance, in an atmosphere of peace and harmony. The castle was even made to survive earthquakes.

Artillery, however, did not usually play an important part in Japanese sieges. Rather than be gunned down by defenders, the besiegers would form a blockade and starve out the inhabitants. In one encounter, the attacking lord, Hideyoshi, passed the time by giving feasts in the surrounding camps, at which dancing girls, musicians and actors entertained. Envious of their merry-making, the castle lord negotiated a peace settlement.

SAMURAI WARRIOR

The Samurai warrior was the Japanese equal of a medieval knight in Europe. He lived in a castle and fought for his daimyo (warlord). Bravery, honor and loyalty were more important than life itself. In defeat, the Samurai chose to kill himself by belly-cutting rather than live on in disgrace.

THE CASTLE MAZE

One of the special methods of fortification the Japanese created was the maze. A complex pattern of corridors and baileys (as shown in the plan, right) fooled the invading enemy about how to find the inner keep. While the attackers were running around confused, Samurai warriors could make surprise ambushes on them.

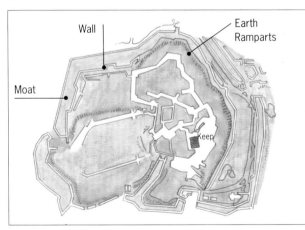

Wall

Earth Ramparts

Moat

Keep

The keep at Himeji Castle was a high, multi-story building, with emperor's quarters at the top. [fan]ciful eaved roofs, with tails of [leap]ing dolphins, create a feeling of [ligh]tness and beauty rather than the [ser]ious business of defense.

Earthquake tremors are common in Japan. Castles there were built in a special way to survive them. The upper structure simply rested on a stone base, allowing it to bounce about during a quake instead of collapsing.

UNIFORM OF THE SAMURAI

The sequence of pictures shows a Samurai warrior dressing for combat. After he performs the ritual washing and shaving of the crown of his head, he puts on silk robes and protective mail armor in readiness to do battle with the enemy.

THE GENIUS OF VAUBAN

The Frenchman Sebastien le Prestre de Vauban (1633-1707) was the greatest military engineer that ever lived. For 200 years his method and system of fortification were used by his successors. By constructing or rebuilding some 60 fortresses around the frontiers of France, he virtually walled in his country, making it the most secure nation in Europe.

By the seventeenth century, the Italians had already made designs to defend against the new heavy artillery: they had replaced circular towers with arrow-shaped bastions, for example. Vauban's genius was not so much in the invention of new designs of fortification, but rather his brilliant use of existing ones to fortify any site. Whether marshland, riverside or hill top, Vauban could fortify it perfectly.

His understanding of the strengths and weaknesses of fortification was so thorough that he was equally clever in attacking cities as defending them. Vauban directed 40 sieges for his king, Louis XIV, and every one was successful.

Sebastien le Prestre de Vauban was the leading military engineer of his time in Europe. As a marshal, he led the French invasion of the Spanish Netherlands and captured Lille. He then fortified the city for his king.

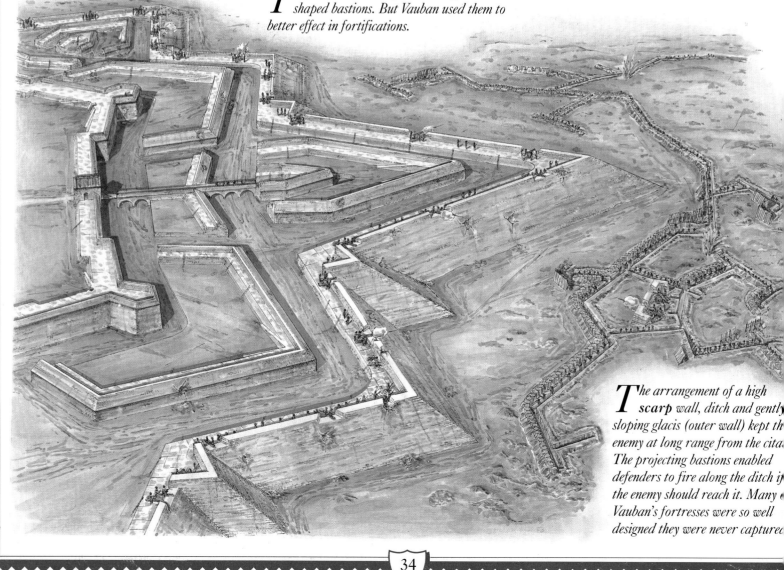

The Italians were the first to design arrow-shaped bastions. But Vauban used them to better effect in fortifications.

The arrangement of a high scarp wall, ditch and gently sloping glacis (outer wall) kept the enemy at long range from the citadel. The projecting bastions enabled defenders to fire along the ditch if the enemy should reach it. Many of Vauban's fortresses were so well designed they were never captured.

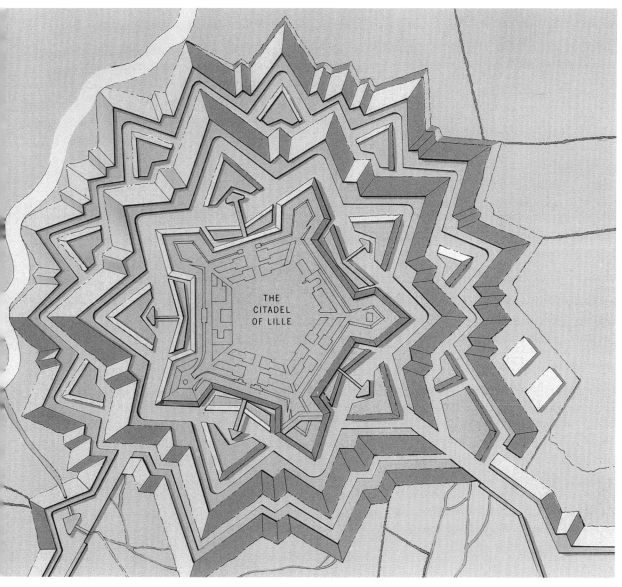

THE
CITADEL
OF LILLE

*T*he most famous of
Vauban's fortifications
were the town and citadel
(shown left) of Lille, begun
in 1668. A vast pentagon
fort enclosed 'a great place,
180 paces across', with a
governor's house, army
barracks, a church and an
arsenal.

*T*he diagram below shows a
cross-section through a typical
Vauban style of fortification.

*A*ngular bastions replaced
round ones because they
were easier to defend. The
diagram above shows the lines
of fire. The round bastions
have 'dead ground' (in red)
where attackers were safe
from defenders' firing.

Firing Platform

Scarp

Revetment

Counterscarp
Revetment

Covered Way

Glacis

Interior of the
fortifications

Ditch

Open Country

THE SAPPER'S ART

*S*oldiers called 'sappers' dig a **trench** and use the
earth to build a **breastwork**. This was a defensive
wall constructed in the field of battle. **Gabions** made
of woven sticks to form a sort of open-ended basket
were moved into position where they were filled with a
combination of packed earth, wood and stone. The
breastwork could be put up quickly during a siege and
used either for defence or attack. It allowed troops to
move about safely while under fire.

THE AMERICAN CIVIL WAR

In February of 1861, seven southern states broke away from the US to form their own new nation, which they called the Confederate States of America. They took control of military camps within their territory, but Fort Sumter, built in Charleston Harbor, South Carolina, refused to surrender. At 4:30 am on April 12th, the first shots of the Civil War were fired when Confederate cannons shelled Fort Sumter.

Four more states joined the South to make 11, against 23 of the North (Union states). As well as being outnumbered by the North, the South had towns with no fortifications. To defend their positions Confederate troops dug trenches in the fields. In as little as 24 hours they could create a long trench system, with rifle pits and mortar (rocket) emplacements. Defenders could defeat a force three times their own size, with few casualties of their own.

Vauban had used trenches in attacking a city in seventeenth-century Europe, but this was the first time they were used extensively in defense. The trench became the common line of defense in warfare, especially during World War I.

Abraham Lincoln (left) was president of the United States on the eve of the Civil War. He sent ammunition and food to Fort Sumter in anticipation of a war. Knowing this, the Confederates started shelling the fort, hoping to force a surrender before the Union supplies arrived.

Fort Sumter was still under construction when war began. It was built on a man-made island in Charleston Harbor, one of several forts made to guard important harbors from attack by sea. It held out for a day and a half before surrendering. During this time the Confederates fired 3,341 shells at it.

New York

STATES OF THE UNION

Petersburg

CONFEDERATE STATES

Fort Sumter

THE ATLANTIC OCEAN

THE UNION-CONFEDERATE DIVIDE

The Confederate States of America were those states in the south which broke away from the Union to form their own separate nation. South Carolina was the first to rebel, in 1860, followed by Mississippi, Florida, Alabama, Georgia, Louisiana and Texas. After the bombardment of Fort Sumter, Virginia, North Carolina, Arkansas and Tennessee joined them. The war ended in 1865, and by 1870 all the rebel states had rejoined the Union.

WAR IN THE TRENCHES

Fort Sedgwick, left, made up just one section of the maze of Petersburg trenches where Union men spent ten months. Most cities had no defenses, so they had to rely on ground fortifications. Mines and booby traps were laid in the field, and **chevaux-des-frises** *(lines of wooden spikes on a beam) slowed down the enemy. Trench mortars (rockets, like short cannons) lobbed shells into enemy trenches. As new positions were won, so troops dug new trench systems: first the rifle pits and stockades for supplies, then trenches were expanded from these. Soldiers like the ones on the right (far right, Confederate; Union, next to him) carried spades and axes in their packs for this purpose.*

THE MAGINOT LINE

The Maginot Line in France was perhaps the most famous fortification for artillery ever built. It was constructed for various reasons: to prevent a war ever being fought on French soil again; to protect the country's industrial areas; and to provide a shield behind which the French army could mobilize its forces. The line was started in 1929 and largely complete by the outbreak of World War II in 1939. It consisted of groups of 'combat blocks' called either *gros ouvrages* or *petits ouvrages* (literally, large works or small works). The larger ones, as the main illustration shows, were like underground villages spread out over a large area. The various parts were often connected by a 60 cm-gauge electric railway. Although electric light and heating were provided, the blocks were often damp and poorly lit.

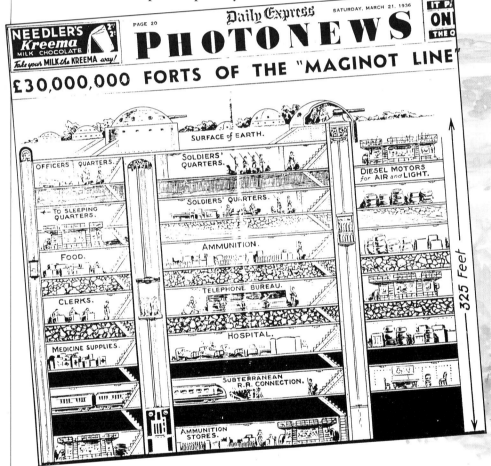

This diagramatic cross-section shows the Maginot Line as it was featured in a popular newspaper in 1936. However, the layout of the fortifications owes more to imagination than to fact.

This cross-section gives an idea of the cramped conditions inside an artillery turret containing a 75 mm gun. Its normal rate of fire was 12 rounds a minute. This could be increased to 24 rounds for short periods.

Cupola

Shell Hoist

Huge power stations generated electricity to operate the underground ventilation, power and lighting systems. Ammunition was stored on lower levels for safety's sake.

It seems that even war did not stop the French soldiers from enjoying their food, which was served with wine on tables that folded down from the tunnel sides when in use.

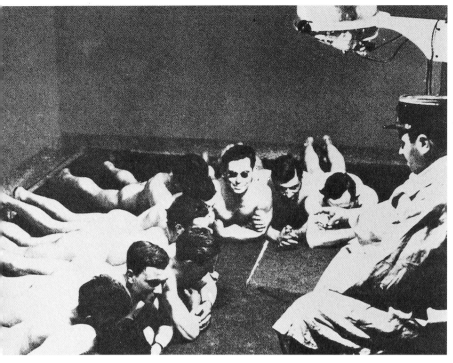

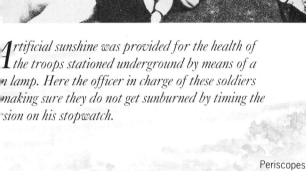

Artificial sunshine was provided for the health of the troops stationed underground by means of a ...n lamp. Here the officer in charge of these soldiers ...making sure they do not get sunburned by timing the ...sion on his stopwatch.

WHY THE PLAN FAILED

The line of the defense was planned to extend along the French and Belgian borders as a protection against the threat of German aggression. But when a real threat of war with Germany came, the Belgians declared themselves a neutral country and so did not build their part of the defenses. As a result, they allowed the invading German army to go around the French part of the Maginot Line.

Garrisons of up to 1,000 soldiers would man the largest of the 'gros ouvrages'. Their living quarters were usually situated some ¹/₂ mile behind the combat blocks and 60-100 feet below the surface.

Fire Control Chamber

Concrete

Periscopes

Gallery

Water Tank

Power Station Exhaust

Electric Ammunition Trolley

Barracks

...nunition Hoist

Ammunition Room

Entrance Gallery

Power Station

The men's sleeping quarters are shown above. Water tanks lay nearer to the surface than the rest of the installation, to create enough pressure for the water to flow properly.

FORTRESS BRITAIN

The nature of warfare was radically different in World War II. Bomber airplanes and fast-moving tanks could easily avoid permanent fortresses. There was now a need to develop smaller fortifications which could cover a large area, and which could not be easily spotted by the enemy.

In preparation for invasion from Germany, Britain built a continuous line of coastal defense from the Humber estuary to Dartmouth. This included 153 anti-aircraft gun batteries; tank traps and wire entanglements placed on the beaches to snare landing enemy tanks; and hundreds of **pill-boxes** both on the coast and inland, under camouflage.

Sea forts were positioned in major river estuaries, such as the Thames and Mersey, to detect, by radar, low-flying aircraft and enemy boats. When sirens wailed to announce an air-raid, people hurried into concrete **bunkers** in their back gardens. In London, during the Blitz of 1940, underground subway stations were used as temporary shelters.

The Blitz of 1940 forced Londoners to take shelter in underground stations during air raids. Many nights were passed uneasily awaiting the outcome. Comics and musicians sometimes entertained to relieve the tension.

LAUNCHING AN ESTUARY FORT

Sea forts were used by the British navy to detect low-flying aircraft approaching Britain. They were made on shore and later taken to the river estuary. Two tug-boats hauled the floating fort into position. Then plugs in the bow were pulled out to allow water into the lowest chamber. The fort slowly sank and came to rest on the sea-bed. Gun **batteries** *and radars equipped the platform, and two pillars provided sleeping quarters and store-rooms.*

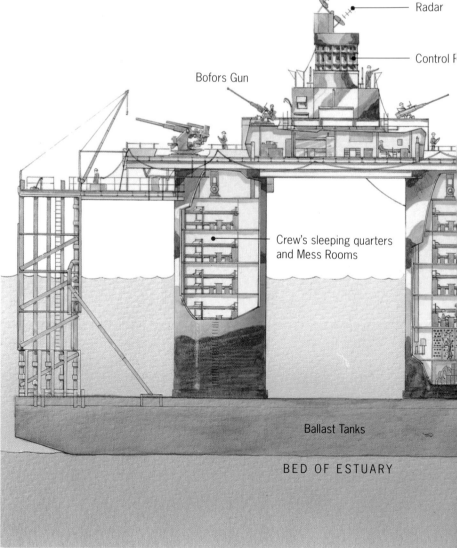

Radar

Control F

Bofors Gun

Crew's sleeping quarters and Mess Rooms

Ballast Tanks

BED OF ESTUARY

DOMESTIC AIR-RAID SHELTERS

More advanced shelters were built by those who could afford them. This fanciful idea shows middle-class suburban dwellers fully prepared for a raid. Inter-connecting chambers and turrets, together with a mechanized air-vent system, give the occupants full protection against a gas attack. Notice the man climbing out of the right turret wears a gas mask. Gas was one of the greatest fears during World War II, after the experience of World War I, when many soldiers died of mustard gas poisoning.

CAMOUFLAGED PILL-BOXES

Camouflage of land defenses was needed to surprise an approachng enemy. This pill-box, cleverly disguised as a pile of logs, guards a railway line.

SEA LEVEL

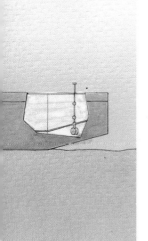

Gun turrets on the sea fort fire at enemy aircraft. The main value of the sea fort, however, was to detect low-flying aircraft which dropped sea mines.

THE NUCLEAR AGE

The invention of the nuclear bomb, which can destroy entire countries, has added a new dimension to war. Nuclear rockets fired from one continent to another must be intercepted before they hit their target. Fortification is no longer made out of concrete, but instead is an invisible 'shield' of computerized technology. Wars of the future might now happen in space.

In 1984, the US government announced a new program of defense technology, nicknamed 'Star Wars'. Radars and telescopes would detect an enemy missile launched thousands of miles away. Laser battle stations based both on earth and in space could direct their powerful beams towards the moving target and destroy it. Alternatively, interceptor rockets could be launched, with computers on board designed to track the enemy missile, and destroy it by colliding with it.

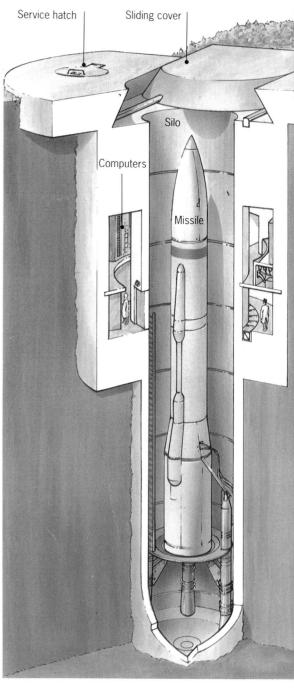

Service hatch | Sliding cover

Silo

Computers

Missile

THE INVISIBLE DEFENSE

Missiles can be launched and guided by computer to strike an enemy rocket. At first, these missiles of defense were based on land. In time, with improved accuracy, nations worried that the enemy could destroy their own rockets. Defenders, therefore, needed to hide their missiles. Some are kept in silos underground (see illustration right), others can be launched from nuclear submarines in the ocean (as shown below). Hundreds of submarines carrying ballistic missiles can patrol the world's oceans, unseen, but ready to launch a missile into orbit if the enemy declares war.

THE ULTIMATE DETERRENT

In the event of a nuclear war, the problem posed to military thinkers is how to withstand the enormous impact of a nuclear bomb. One idea was the construction of an underground missile silo, shown above. This is a tube-shaped chamber holding a rocket. The silo is made of dense concrete to resist the shock of a nuclear explosion. Bunkers to the side protect launch crews and the computer equipment that is needed to guide the missile to its destination. These silos, however, do not give enough protection against the most powerful bombs.

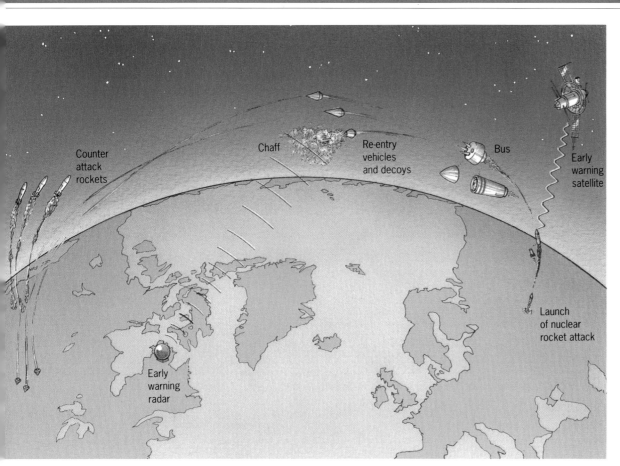

Counter attack rockets

Chaff

Re-entry vehicles and decoys

Bus

Early warning satellite

Launch of nuclear rocket attack

Early warning radar

SATELLITE WAR

Satellites in space can detect nuclear rockets launched by an enemy from another continent. A 'bus' (see left) carries the warheads into space and then fires them. It also releases dust-like chaff to confuse defensive radars on earth which are trying to track the missiles. These great dome-shaped radars, such as those at Fylingdales in Yorkshire (shown below), are located along the Arctic Circle between North America and Russia. Defensive missiles are launched from undergound or submarine (see far left), and guided by computer to strike the enemy warheads in space, well before they reach their targets.

GLOSSARY

BAILEY: courtyard inside a castle compound. Introduced by the Normans when they invaded England and built *motte-and-bailey* style castles

BARBICAN: the fortified gatehouse of a castle or *citadel*

BARRACK: sleeping quarters for soldiers in an army camp

BASTION: a defensive tower, usually low, attached to the main wall of a fortress, but projecting in front of it. It can be rounded, angular, or pentagonal

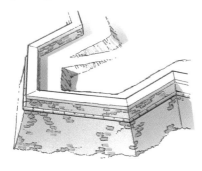

BATTERY: a platform, usually protected by a *parapet* - for cannons and guns

BATTLEMENT: the fortified top of a castle wall and tower

BREACH: a gap blown open in a wall of a fortress by a mine or artillery fire

BREASTWORK: a wall built to breast height for defense in the field

BUNKER: an underground hiding place that gives protection from bombs or artillery fire

CASEMATE: a chamber built in a thick wall and used as a gun position or as a store-room

CHEVAUX-DES-FRISES: horizontal beams with wooden spikes built to stop advancing soldiers

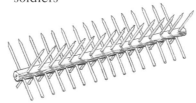

CITADEL: a fortress built to protect a town

COVERED WAY : the path below a *parapet* which enables troops to move into position without being exposed to enemy fire

CURTAIN WALL: the main wall of a castle, usually between two towers

DITCH: a wide, dry *trench* dug outside a fortress wall

DRAWBRIDGE: a bridge over a *moat* at the gate of a castle. It can be raised to prevent an enemy from entering the castle

EMBRASURE: an opening cut in a *parapet* or a wall for guns to fire through; also called a crenel

GABION: a basket which is filled with earth during *trench*-digging, and used as a shield against gunfire

GATEHOUSE: a building at the gate of a fortress, where the guard normally lives

GLACIS: the first outer bank or wall of a fortification, gently sloping away from the *parapet* and *covered way* at an angle of less than 45°, the purpose of which is to expose an attacker to defensive fire

KEEP: the last defensible part of a castle

LINE OF DEFENSE: the line of fire from the side of a *bastion* (A) along the face of the next *bastion* (F)

LOOP HOLE: thin vertical opening in a castle tower. It provides light, and allows defenders in the tower to see out and to shoot arrows or fire guns

MACHICOLATION: a structure hanging over the top of a wall. It allows defenders to drop missiles on attackers at the foot of the wall

MAGAZINE: the place or building for the storage of arms, ammunition and provisions

MOAT: a water-filled *ditch* or lake surrounding a fortress

MOTTE: the Norman word for a mound, inside a castle compound, on which was built the *keep*

OUTWORK: a defensive structure placed outside a fortress

PALISADE: a wooden fence, or wall usually placed at the top of a *rampart*. It is made of a series of wooden stakes with pointed ends as an early form of defensive wall

PARAPET: a low wall at the top of a tower or main wall, giving shelter to defenders

PILL-BOX: a concrete shelter from which defenders can fire at an approaching enemy

PORTCULLIS: a large wooden or iron grating which can be lowered or raised behind a castle gate or *drawbridge*

RAMPART: a thick wall of earth forming the main defense of a fort

RAVELIN: a triangular *bastion* in front of the main wall

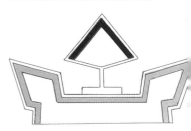

SCARP: the high wall of a Renaissance fort that lies behind a *ditch* and lower *glacis* wall

TALUS: a wall that slopes outwards in medieval forts

TRENCH: a deep *ditch* dug in the field to give soldiers protection from enemy fire

WATCHTOWER: a tower in the main wall of a fort from which guards can look out for enemy approach

Project editor: Thomas Keegan
Art director: Nigel Soper
Consultant: Professor Simon Pepper PhD RIBA, University of Liverpool
Editor: Diana Russell
Picture research: Diana Morris
Illustrations: Maltings Partnership, Michael White - Temple Rogers,
Photos: p.8 Zefa, p.10-11 Alan Sorrell British Museum, p.12 Zefa, p.28 Mansell Collection, The Tank Museum, p.38 Daily Express, p.39 Ministère d'Etat chargé de la Défense Nationale, Paris, p.40, 41 Imperial War Museum, p.43 John Donat.